Rock the Boat

Robert Miltner

All Nations Press

Copyright 2005 Robert Miltner

All Rights Reserved. This book, or parts thereof, may not be reproduced in any form without permission.

Rock the Boat

Library of Congress Card Catalogue Information on Reserve

ISBN 0-9725110-3-2

First Edition

All Nations Press
PO Box 601
White Marsh, VA 23183
www.allnationspress.com

For Lisa

Acknowledgements

The author wishes to thank the following publications in which some of these poems, often in different versions and with various titles, first appeared.

Chiron Review: "Dinner Date with Anna Freud"

CrossConnect: "A Brief History of Cairn Markers" and "Sunday Drivers"

Free Lunch: "Our Own Cooking Show"

Into the Teeth of the Wind: "Outside the Smithsonian"

key satch(el): "Momentum" and "The Lass of Aughrim Variations"

NEOAnthology: "La Pensione: A Romance" and "Safety Limits"

Potion: "Rock the Boat" and "Rockville"

The Prose Poem: An International Journal: "Shoebox"

Sleeping Fish: "Playing the Role of You"

Stray Dog: "Pyromania: A Love Story"

The Vincent Brothers Review: "Strays"

Whiskey Island: "Wichita Winter"

About the cover: "Rock the Boat" by Marc Snyder. Marc Snyder is a printmaker living in Hamden, Connecticut. He has a Master of Fine Arts degree in printmaking from Indiana University and a Bachelors degree in studio art from the University of Virginia. His prints and artist's books are available through his Fiji Island Mermaid Press, http://www.fimp.net

"I was born to rock the boat"
—Warren Zevon

"Oh no, don't you rock my boat!"
—Bob Marley

Contents

Safety Limits   8

Yahudi   9

Report Card   10

Strays   11

Rock the Boat   12

Playing the Role of *You*   13

Dying in Alphabetical Order   14

Rockville   15

Snow Bound   16

How Can I Describe It?   17

Pyromania: A Love Story   18

Sunday Mornings over Coffee   19

La Pensione: A Romance   20

Our Own Cooking Show   23

Dinner Date with Anna Freud   24

The Lass of Aughrim Variations   25

A Brief History of Cairn Markers   26

Sunday Drivers   27

Shoebox   28

Closing In on Closing Out   29

Outside the Smithsonian   30

Card Day   31

Momentum   32

Safety Limits

Ice forms first near the shore, where water is shallow, then extends out toward the middle where it meets, smooth as chrome. *Careful,* the parents call out to their children, *you can never catch that horizon you are chasing.* But the children's eyes are wide as the sky.

Skates on, the kids glide toward the glazed center. *Watch out,* the parents explain, *what looks solid could be as thin as a razor blade; you cold fall like a coin into an arcade game.* Their coats open like boat sails, the kids are blown by the wind like dead leaves; their tomorrows stretch like string.

Blue, the curtain draped and hanging, white, the distance blurring the lake's horizon. *Beware,* the parents warn, *that border between what's solid and what's air is a wound, a suture, a scar, a mirror's crack.* But the boys and girls are lifting, rising like kites.

Yahudi

My brothers, cousins, and I used to crawl around on the floor playing, lost in a land of small cars and trucks. If one of us noticed our Grandma Ethel sitting on her davenport, her eyes would suddenly look up from *The Cleveland Press*, stare past us toward the staircase, and she'd exclaim, "Look, there he is!"

Our small heads would spin around like gyroscopes, but we would only see the staircase, the landing, the leaded glass window. "Did you see him?" Ethel would ask us with a laugh, "It's Yahudi, the little man who wasn't there!"

But we didn't see him. Or did we? Didn't my cousin Danny claim to catch a glimpse of a left foot? Didn't my brother Ken say he saw a shadow scurrying on the wall beyond the railing?

Yahudi, hoarder of mislaid toys. Yahudi, pickpocket of lost socks. Yahudi, stealer of unwary children. Yahudi, owner of runaway dogs.

He was never there. Was he? Quick, look up! Did you see him this time? What was that slip of a shadow you caught out of the corner of your eye? Better take stock: maybe something is missing from *your* life.

Yahudi, larcenist of first loves. Yahudi, embezzler of innocence. Yahudi, burglar of family intimacy. Yahudi, the little man who wasn't there.

Report Card

Your son is not working up to his potential

If you could see the intelligence tests and achievement tests he has completed, you would not accept these marks

This is not the first time I've had to speak to him about this

His daydreaming has become chronic

I know he can do better and believe the next six weeks will prove it

His scores suffer because he does not seem to check his work before turning it in

He is listening harder and his attitude seems better, thus I am still hoping for improvement

Your son's effort has surely slackened and is reflected in his grades

A non-conformist par excellence, no matter what he is told to do, he comes up with the annoying habit of offering a substitute "just as good"

Although bright and a top reader, he seems misdirected

There are times when he refuses to accept the assignment, then reconsiders and goes ahead the right way

Please talk with your son and encourage him from your end

A little non-conformity is very good, but his is too much

His nose is always buried in the wrong book

We are no doubt mutually concerned about the kind of career your son might find in the future

Strays

Ropes to boats, stairs to airplanes, the dirigible drops its ballast, fires up the burners, rises. *Get down!* barks the owner to the won't-listen dog. Water bowl turned over. Fix the dog to calm it down and all the dog will want to do is eat.

Lost dogs often languish in cinderblock buildings before being put down. Even their loss won't lift. Turned over to the county kennel for adoption, no ropes to walk these dogs, no door to bark by. Degrees of compassion are comparable to stairs or stars, rowboats or oceanliners.

At the hot air balloon show, one figure is a doghouse, one a hot dog, one a dog. The ropes loosened, the balloon dog starts to float away. One step beyond the rope, and it will have known more than one home. Will have gone where the bone is buried or the boat is adrift.

Rock the Boat

I dock and meet the woman from Islaroja. We sit at her kitchen table drinking red wine and eating peppermint ice cream. Our tongues burn. Desire is our boat.

All night we row hard against the tides. Our shirts are soaked and sticking to our skin. Rain gathers in our mouths. At dawn, the boat wrecks on the Coast.

The wind off the bay is hot, close. An ibis steps out from the calla lilies, disappears under a palmetto palm. Moths open and close their wings like pliers. We are beyond repair.

Playing the Role of *You*

We can imagine our own death. Jumping off the ledge, hurling ourselves in front of a speeding truck, igniting ourselves as a noble protest against some ignoble cause: we can, and we do. But we cannot dream ourselves dying.

At the moment before the avalanche engulfs, before the dog pack attacks, we wake up, hearts pounding, throats so dry we don't dare swallow for fear our esophagus will shatter, its sound like windows being blown out from a drive-by shooting.

If we dream in color, we can actually see the blood, red as when we force our eyes shut against the summer sun, though we know that it's no more real than an actor's prop, a magician's trick, a sideshow gimmick.

In the morning, in the shower, our heads under the faucet, we remember still shots from the dream, like a collage of lingering movie images. And, eyes closed, we don't see the swirl of red spinning clockwise down the drain.

Dying in Alphabetical Order

The obituaries reveal that my old math teacher died. Though it didn't say she'd *died*; it said instead she'd *passed away*. As she did. As we all do, sooner than later. As I too will do. And you: pass. Life passing us by, passing on, after we've passed through. More than a passing thought, this idea of passing over into the next life, if there is one. Hell, I remember in her seventh grade algebra class, failing to discern the lowest common denominator. Standing at the blackboard, the numbers and letters like the Rosetta Stone, and me thinking, *I'm dying up here!* Back then, all I wanted to do was pass.

Rockville

What a tree's roots grasp and hoard makes a mountain. Exposed, the mountain is boulder, cairn, wall; buried, it is challenge: *drill down, then,* it taunts. No fool to grasp a pick-axe, of course, and devote his life to lost causes, the wise man will walk away, seeking dark bottom lands, wide meadows, flat as-far-as-the-eye-can-see fields. For him, rocks ruin the plow, are at best a grave's friend.

Instead, he will live in one of those small towns comfortable as night lights along the turnpike, places where we stop to buy gas and talk over a coke while waiting for change. When we say *skyscraper,* in his skyblue eyes he will picture a grain elevator. When we say *mountain,* he will look down in mouth-open wonder at the closest stone.

Snowbound

During the earlier months I played myself at checkers just to get up and move to the other side of the table. Then I realized winning and losing are a coin with only one side.

The clock's slow tick leaves me unsure what's told: today, tomorrow, yesterday, same. I can't recall why it makes any difference.

I've given up reading the few books I own; the letters on the page turn into too many crows in a snow-covered field where I plow and sow my dreams.

All that remains are shavings that I use for tinder in the small Franklin stove, for by now I've whittled an ark-full of animals, though most folks lack the faculties to recognize, let alone accept, the creatures I create.

See: here's a tiger with teeth like plows. This one's an elephant with the head of a combine. And look: here's a horse with a barn for its body.

How Can I Describe It?

It was Robert Mapplethorpe meets *Lord of the Flies.* Norman Rockwell meets *Pulp Fiction.* Jackson Pollack meets *Gentlemen Prefer Blondes.* Claude Monet meets *The Bride of Frankenstein.* Rene Magritte meets *The Maltese Falcon.* Salvador Dali meets *Bambi.* It was Marcel DuChamp meets *Rear Window.* It was Andy Warhol meets *It's a Wonderful Life.*

Pyromania: A Love Story

His desire is gasoline, her dream a flame. He cracks boxes, stokes wood, pokes ashes. Sparks ignite the tinder of her lips, crackle the kindling of her kisses. With each whisper, each breath, the embers glow brighter.

Audible to her ear alone is the impulse, the insistence in his voice. This is the kind of air on which she thrives, the kind of fire he feeds.

By moonlight, matchlight, candlelight, firelight, he loves to watch her dance. With the cool beauty of blue flames, she starts to move. First she is the yellow of ballet, soon the orange of a sultry tango, next the bright red of swing, then the pulsing throb of a colorful nightclub crowd which, excited by its own force, bursts out of the doors and starts dancing in the streets.

His breath is like a bellows as his cheeks redden, inflaming the glow of his telltale face until, sudden as a siren, he recedes to the anonymity of the shadows. He is wallblender, she is the star under the stage lights. Only his eyes continue to hold her fire.

And when it all comes down to ashes, as it always does, she will again be lye. He'll boil water. Then scrub his hands until the friction makes his skin burn.

Sunday Mornings Over Coffee

These are the weekends of our new love. We remember everything just as we imagined it would be.

We dawdle over fresh fruit, dip our croissants in the sweetness of the past, the sugar foregrounded in the fresh-ground coffee.

Last week the news arrived again. It was bleak, black, brick. Each time we fold a section of the newspaper, get the mail, it's a landfill.

Holding hands, we hear the siren surprise of the ambulance, the metallic whine of another jet from the airport, each with a place reserved for us.

La Pensione: A Romance

That spring we thought we could add some spice to our relationship. A little cooking, a little stirring.

Vito Presti, "Mister Italy," had the best price for eight days and seven nights, accommodations and air fare included.

The place we stayed was a second floor walk up run by a Sicilian grandmother named Anna who dreamed of dark chocolate, former lovers, biscotti, and grandchildren.

The restaurant felt more like a large kitchen in a home.

The tour takes you up in the mountains to the edge of the local volcano, which is still active.

All over Perugia there are houses with fake painted windows.

In Verona, they brought us a dish with calamari called *Romeo's Lips* which is served with a dry red wine called *Juliet's Nurse*.

You sat on the stone wall. Your legs looked like two straws drinking from the fountain below the marble archangel by the old cathedral. You hadn't said a word since dinner, and frankly, I wasn't expecting you to.

After all that comes together, the spices are added.

As the moon rose over the bay above the small fishing boats, I smoked those French cigarettes that smelled like cloves and drank the cheap local Chianti from the lips of a basketed bottle. I was struck dumb, my mouth open wider than a canal, as I realized you held more secrets than the vaults at the Vatican.

After the olive oil is heated, the chef said, *add two cloves of garlic, a handful of fresh basil, uncut, and three seeded tomatoes, then cook for two minutes before adding the shrimp just long enough for them to pink.* And, he added, wagging his finger at us like a celery stalk, *serve it over angel-hair pasta, or don't serve it at all.*

Then the lid goes on, and the whole thing simmers.

In Venice, our gondoliers wore polyester striped shirts with soiled white slacks and sang cheesy Italian versions of American pop songs. You wore your orange faux tam, but you looked a bit green around the gills, I thought, from the way the boat lurched, while I had indigestion from all that garlic on the roasted artichokes we'd had for lunch.

The responsibility for the recipe rests squarely on the shoulders of the pastry chef.

Coming from the same biological family, the rose, which has become a symbol for all flowers, is similar to the apple, which has become the symbol for all fruits.

Many of the ancient stone structures have collapsed. Some from violence, some from stress.

During Lent, almonds and vanilla make the best cakes. You can get a good price in the market for them. In the piazza, we watched the old men dunk the cakes in sweet wine.

Since a weather front was moving through, and the morning's showers were still lurking about, we had to cancel the car.

Your hair fell across your face. The moon light coming in from the open door to the balcony fell across your face. Your shadow fell across me on the bed. I was wondering how to say *done* in Italian.

Our Own Cooking Show

The large pot, filled with water, is on the stove, turned up to *high*.

I hold two plump tomatoes, lower them gently into the water. Your hand cradles a sweet Italian sausage, ready to add.

Bay leaf I put in, a bit of basil, a pinch of thyme. You sprinkle in sea salt, ground pepper, oregano.

The onion skins are like wrapping paper I remove from gifts; my hands will retain their scent until morning. Your hands lift a zucchini from the counter; washed, trimmed, it too goes into the soup.

Once I remove the skin from the garlic close like gloves from fingers. I admire what is revealed. You grasp carrots one by one, stroking them slowly down to wet shafts.

Our eyes meet. Our fingers brush as we reach for our glasses of Pinot Grigio, and we drink. Our eyes meet again.

On the stove, the water begins to boil. It boils. And keeps on boiling.

Dinner Date with Anna Freud

Tenderly she fingers the spoon, cooing sounds coming from her throat; slowly she licks the slow honey, loving the feel of the cool curve against her moistening tongue.

The next utensil she just looks at, picks it up as she would a dead bird, shifts her fork from cutlery to verb.

Last the knife is firmly grasped; she holds it erect, rasps, *Father*, and thrusts it into a piece of steak. Then she cuts, cuts, cuts, cuts.

The Lass of Aughrim Variations
for James Joyce

He asks himself: what is a woman standing on the stairs in the shadow, listening to distant music, a symbol of?

He asks himself: what is a shadow? Listens to the distant woman. Feels her hand along the railing.

A lute can be heard nearby, the musician obscured by shadows. The music is as distant from the hearer as from the musician.

Her hair is the cat in the shadow: listen. He asks himself: distant?

He asks himself: suppose he was the stair and her feet the shadow, her sensual immediacy a symbol of the opposite of distant music?

He asks himself: what if a lute is a symbol of a woman? Listens to the distant music. The cat makes a sound like a lute string from the staircase.

He asks the woman to listen to the distant symbol. He asks himself: shadow? The woman listens to how the stairs shadow, but wonders to where. How often must distant sound be heard.

Listens to the cat stand, feels its standing, imagines the *what next*; the shadow. Feels the shadowcat descent the steps, symbol of distant longing. Of course a cat would descent the shadowed stairs. He asks himself: what if a cat is a symbol of a woman?

Which is the symbol of himself: the shadow or the stairs?

He asks himself: listen to the distant shadow? He asks himself: what is listen a symbol of?

Shadows and recesses of the winding staircase. A black cat moves shadow to light, symbol to light, shadow to symbol, downward.

A Brief History of Cairn Markers

Each consequence is written in water; each inconsequence codified in stone. Rocks and bones have been murdered and museumed. The arboretum had its heartwood sold for pamphlets to promote what it was before it lost its soul.

Spirits I always considered an odd word for alcohol–it means *ghosts*, yes?– before I stole some whiskey from my father's liquor cabinet and drank it in the woods, camping one summertime, and I was possessed of a spirit all right *that* night!

Evening does not descend. Darkness does not fall. Dusk does not close some curtain. Death's second self does not seal up all the rest. Sleeping deeply is a gift given to deceive those who have not yet overthrown their fathers.

The sun's light clarifies the intransigence– which we think of as a form of action–that moves quicker than glacial deposits. Purse your lips when you hold a stone to throw or listen to. What do you hear? The witch of rose hips, a boulder on her belly, drowning to prove her innocence.

Sunday Drivers

Newly spread manure smells fertile, seems as honest as sweat in the just plowed and joyous fields; soybean farmers especially are quite excited to be getting on with such sprouting this spring.

No trains run on rails rusting from continuous disuse on discontinued routes, no freight, no conductor to wave to the children playing in the haymows.

Never have we seen such an eyeful; everything that ever even minimally flowered is maxed-out this year: pinkwhite and yellow and whitepink and red and whitepurple and green background and then all around is more, more, so much more.

No squared corner in the pole barn, no lazy dog, no barn owl nobody gives a hoot in hell about.

Now the motorists, driving into the country to get a good deal on antiques, say, *My, isn't that what-do-you-call-it pretty?* as they push the button on the cruise control.

No June picnics or brides, no ice cream socials in a month of endless comets' tails. No one's catching lightning bugs this June.

Nearby, on the county road adjacent, motorists roll up their minivan windows, pop in another CD, flick the button to *ON* on their AC.

Shoebox

The land curves. The land is continual.

Continue.

The land curves and rounds and rolls and the land contours and curves and climbs and unwinds. The land continuously curves along. Curving continuously the curved land rolls.

Continue.

Earthmovers move mechanically earth: gash. Hole. Then girder, girder, beam, panel, roof, scaffolding. Construction as destruction. Lights intrude upon nocturnal land curves, land black as blacktop for cars to park on. The rectangle wrecks the tangle of trees.

All around rollingly the land continuously curves.

Continue.

Closing In on Closing Out

A father leaves, moves out, moves on, moves away. The boy, in the woods where the autumn leaves glaze the landscape gold, is like a puppy, pushing, roughing. Walking back home, the boy transforms, grows, outgrows his worn-out shoes. Inside, he finds a frayed shirt in the back of a closet, puts it on, and hears his father's voice from his chest, near the heart: in his head is a desert, in his heart it rains.

The boy doesn't know the world is always calling, doesn't hear the phone ring or the bird call or the church bell. He stands framed in the doorway, looking out at the uncertain Ohio sky. He feels the wind come through the screen, watches the rain slap against the window glass. The boy remembers the words his grandfather gave: *Wear a large coat and layer your clothes; you'll stay dry through the storm.*

Outside the Smithsonian

Four Buddhist monks walking, orange gold gold orange, eight white socks and sandals, passing through a stone's hole like a copper key, turning the tumblers to open Nirvana. They make me wish I was monk number five.

A group of tourists, dressed to match their digital cameras, tells their children to *Quit your bickering.* As a diversion, they point to a magnolia tree covered in white cups and tell the children to *Look at the cherry blossoms.*

Some huge guy under a cowboy hat, shiny big-ass Harley-Davidson belt buckle, asks me which of the buildings has the stuffed dodo in it. I send him to the one where I remember seeing a large mirror.

The middle-aged man, seated on the bench across from me, with his notebook open and his pen in his hand, is writing in his journal: *Four Buddhist monks walking.*

Card Day

What a cute *Happy Divorce Day* card you think as you open the envelope, discovering you have the kind of marriage retailers sell greeting cards for: *Sweetest Day, Valentine's Day, Tenth Anniversary of Your Wedding Day*, all the appropriate props culled from on-line catalogues till you're knee-deep in credit cards, monthly payments hanging like stones around your neck, *New Couch Day, Microwave Replacement Day, Different Carpeting for the Family Room Day, Let's Buy a New Minivan Day*, the picket fence out front like a smile to the world: straight and even and white as the kids' teeth after the braces are taken off and paid off, *Final Payment to the Orthodontist Day, Good-bye Retainer Day, Time to Schedule a Fluoride Treatment Day*, dinners when the talk is all how-was-your-day? And who-called? And did-you-see-that-thing-in-the-paper? *New Coat of Paint on the Porch Rail Day, Cut the Chemlawned Grass Day, Stain and Seal the Deck Day*, but never real questions, those unspoken, the eyes not meeting, no conveyance of the real feelings: *Normal Chit-chat Day, What a Clever Mask Day, Cover Your Heart in Paper Hats Day*.

Momentum

Is like going off on a tangent, like an optimistic return to the intersection in a parallel galaxy, like the fastest loop-de-loop on the newest roller coaster at the just-revamped amusement park, spilling you dizzy right back to where you started from, getting at the end of the line only to see someone who looks like you simultaneously the first up, ready, holding the ticket you gave to yourself getting off the ride at the moment you were getting on.

Card Day

What a cute *Happy Divorce Day* card you think as you open the envelope, discovering you have the kind of marriage retailers sell greeting cards for: *Sweetest Day, Valentine's Day, Tenth Anniversary of Your Wedding Day*, all the appropriate props culled from on-line catalogues till you're knee-deep in credit cards, monthly payments hanging like stones around your neck, *New Couch Day, Microwave Replacement Day, Different Carpeting for the Family Room Day, Let's Buy a New Minivan Day*, the picket fence out front like a smile to the world: straight and even and white as the kids' teeth after the braces are taken off and paid off, *Final Payment to the Orthodontist Day, Good-bye Retainer Day, Time to Schedule a Fluoride Treatment Day*, dinners when the talk is all how-was-your-day? And who-called? And did-you-see-that-thing-in-the-paper? *New Coat of Paint on the Porch Rail Day, Cut the Chemlawned Grass Day, Stain and Seal the Deck Day*, but never real questions, those unspoken, the eyes not meeting, no conveyance of the real feelings: *Normal Chit-chat Day, What a Clever Mask Day, Cover Your Heart in Paper Hats Day*.

Momentum

Is like going off on a tangent, like an optimistic return to the intersection in a parallel galaxy, like the fastest loop-de-loop on the newest roller coaster at the just-revamped amusement park, spilling you dizzy right back to where you started from, getting at the end of the line only to see someone who looks like you simultaneously the first up, ready, holding the ticket you gave to yourself getting off the ride at the moment you were getting on.